Electric Vehicles

Lesley Ward

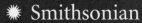

Smithsonian

D1386898

Contributing Author

Heather Schultz, M.A.

Consultants

Roger White
Museum Curator, Division of Work and Industry
National Museum of American History

Tamieka Grizzle, Ed.D.
K–5 STEM Lab Instructor
Harmony Leland Elementary School

Stephanie Anastasopoulos, M.Ed.
TOSA, STREAM Integration
Solana Beach School District

Publishing Credits

Rachelle Cracchiolo, M.S.Ed., *Publisher*
Conni Medina, M.A.Ed., *Managing Editor*
Diana Kenney, M.A.Ed., NBCT, *Series Developer*
Véronique Bos, *Creative Director*
June Kikuchi, *Content Director*
Robin Erickson, *Art Director*
Seth Rogers, *Editor*
Mindy Duits, *Senior Graphic Designer*
Smithsonian Science Education Center

Image Credits: front cover, p.1 Scharfsinn/Shutterstock; p.5 (top) Lucas Jackson/Reuters/ Newscom; p.6 (bottom) General Motors/KRT/Newscom; p.7 (top) Paolo Bona/Shutterstock; p.9 (top) VintageMedStock/Alamy; p.9 (bottom) Public domain; p.10 © Smithsonian; p.11 (top) Everett Historical/Shutterstock; p.11 (bottom) Grzegorz Czapski/Shutterstock; p.13 (top) Testing/ Shutterstock; p.15 (top) Bettmann/Getty Images; p.15 (bottom) Vilius Steponenas/Shutterstock; p.17 (top) Adam Berry/Getty Images; p.17 (bottom) Marius Dobilas/Shutterstock; p.19 (top) Christopher Marsh/Alamy; p.19 (bottom) Sjo/iStock; p.20 WENN Ltd/Alamy; p.21 (top) Sjoerd van der Wal/iStock; p.21 (bottom) Elon Musk via Twitter; p.24 (bottom) Patrick T. Fallon/Bloomberg via Getty Images; pp.24–25 Taina Sohlman/Shutterstock; p.26 Erkan Atbas/Shutterstock; p.27 Radu Razvan/Shutterstock; p.28 360b/Shutterstock; p.31 Oleg Znamenskiy/Shutterstock; all other images iStock and/or Shutterstock.

Library of Congress Cataloging-in-Publication Data

Names: Ward, Lesley, author.
Title: Electric vehicles / Lesley Ward.
Description: Huntington Beach, CA : Teacher Created Materials, [2019] | Includes index. | Audience: Grade 4 to 6. |
Identifiers: LCCN 2018005461 (print) | LCCN 2018026652 (ebook) | ISBN 9781493869428 (E-book) | ISBN 9781493867028 (pbk.)
Subjects: LCSH: Electric vehicles--Juvenile literature.
Classification: LCC TL220 (ebook) | LCC TL220 .W368 2019 (print) | DDC 629.22/93--dc23
LC record available at https://lccn.loc.gov/2018005461

Teacher Created Materials

5301 Oceanus Drive
Huntington Beach, CA 92649-1030
www.tcmpub.com

ISBN 978-1-4938-6702-8

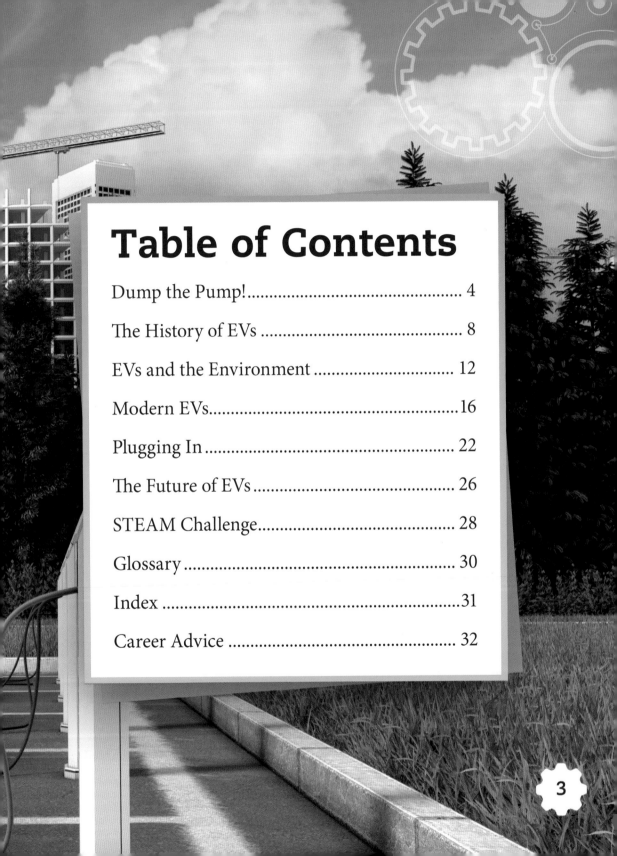

Table of Contents

Dump the Pump!... 4

The History of EVs 8

EVs and the Environment 12

Modern EVs...16

Plugging In 22

The Future of EVs 26

STEAM Challenge... 28

Glossary 30

Index 31

Career Advice 32

Dump the Pump!

Your family's car is running low on fuel. You need to head for the nearest gas station—and quick! Right? Nope. Instead, your parents drive to your house, pull into the garage, and park. They grab the big plug attached to the charging station by a cord and insert it into the **port** on the car.

After about six to eight hours, the car's battery is fully charged, and your family is ready to get back on the road. No need to buy expensive gasoline or waste time in line waiting for the next available pump. Why? Because you have an electric vehicle, or EV!

EVs are a common sight on the road today. Just like a cell phone, an EV runs on a lithium-ion battery that can be charged over and over. Early EVs were easy to spot. But today, many EVs are luxurious vehicles that drive just like gasoline-powered cars. It's hard to tell them apart, just as carmakers planned.

The Rimac Concept One is one of the most expensive EVs in the world. It can be yours for only $980,000!

EVs are becoming popular with drivers around the world. EV owners don't worry about the rising price of gasoline. They don't take their cars to repair shops to change the oil. EVs are cheaper to drive than cars that use gasoline.

EVs appeal to people who are concerned about climate change. They are **emission**-free vehicles. They don't **spew** smelly exhaust from their tailpipes. In fact, EVs don't even have tailpipes!

Car exhaust is made of gases that create smog and air pollution. It also contains carbon monoxide, a greenhouse gas. Greenhouse gases cause a buildup of heat in the atmosphere. Scientists have found that this heat results in global warming. Global warming is the big change in Earth's weather patterns. It has a negative effect on Earth's **ecosystems**.

A lot of people want to protect the environment. They are switching to EVs to do just that. There are many EVs for people to choose from.

The General Motors EV1 was the first mass-produced electric vehicle.

Greenhouse gases from cars that run on gasoline stay in the air for years after they are released.

The History of EVs

The main mode of transport in the early 1800s had four legs, a mane, and a tail. It was a horse! Horses carried riders. They pulled carts. Horses were strong, but they had their limits. They also needed to be fed and cared for. People knew there had to be a way to power a cart without using a horse.

In 1800, batteries were invented. They created power in the form of an electrical current. Scientists thought that battery power could be used to replace horsepower.

Robert Anderson, a Scottish inventor, built one of the first EVs in the 1830s. He attached a battery to a motor. The motor turned the wheels of a cart.

Anderson's "horseless carriage" was **crude**. It rolled just a few feet. The battery could only be used once. But his work inspired many inventors who heard of his work.

One of the first successful American EVs was built in 1890. A chemist named William Morrison designed it. It ran on 24 batteries that could be recharged. Morrison showed the car at the 1893 World's Fair in Chicago. He used it to give rides to **VIPs**. It was a big hit with the crowds.

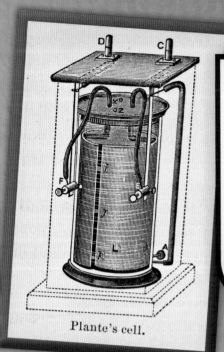

Plante's cell.

Lead-Acid Batteries

Gaston Planté (gas-TAHN plan-TAY) was a physics professor in France. He invented an electric storage battery in 1859. His battery could be recharged. He separated two sheets of lead with rubber. The lead was rolled into spirals. He connected the spirals to metal terminals. Then, he put the spirals into a glass container with sulfuric acid. The battery made a charge of two volts.

Morrison's 1890 electric carriage

9

The first EV that people could buy went on sale in 1894. It was called the Electrobat. It was designed by an engineer named Henry Morris and a chemist named Pedro Salom. It could drive 40 kilometers (25 miles) on one battery charge. It drove at speeds up to 32 kilometers per hour (20 miles per hour). It won races against other EVs.

Many of the cars on the road were EVs in the early 1900s. Most of the taxis in New York City used batteries. But EVs were expensive. They cost around $2,000. A horse only cost $100. For many people at that time, $2,000 was more money than they earned in four years.

The American **industrialist** Henry Ford produced a new car in 1908. It was called the Model T. It was powered by gasoline. The Model T made a lot of noise. It spewed black smoke. But it cost only $850. EVs just couldn't compete with the price of the Model T. It would be many years before people became interested in EVs again.

A family rides in an electric vehicle around 1900.

Thomas Edison bought an EV in 1899. There wa[s]
one big problem—he didn't know how to drive!

Thomas Edison

Ford M[odel T]

EVs and the Environment

EVs have become more popular recently. A lot of people want to drive cars that do not harm the environment. They want to reduce air pollution, which is caused when man-made waste is dumped into the air. Air pollution is caused by things such as factories, steel mills, and oil refineries. Chemicals come out of their smokestacks. These chemicals can cause **cancer** and other diseases.

Cars and trucks that use gas also make air pollution. Their exhaust contains carbon monoxide and carbon dioxide. These chemicals cause health problems, such as asthma. Pollutants in the air can also cause acid rain. Acid rain damages trees and crops. It hurts wildlife. It poisons lakes and kills fish.

Cars pollute in other ways, too. Gasoline spills and oil leaks release **toxins** into the ground and water.

Other pollutants travel into the atmosphere. They cause the ozone layer to thin. Ozone is a natural gas made of oxygen. It shields Earth from the sun's rays. When the ozone layer gets thinner, Earth gets hotter.

Smog from air pollution can be seen in the air.

In many cities around the world, people protect their lungs from smog by wearing masks when they are outside.

Burning **fossil fuels** is one of the main causes of global warming. Gasoline is a fossil fuel. It is refined from oil. When it is used in a car's engine, it gives off greenhouse gases, such as carbon dioxide. These gases trap heat from the sun on Earth. This causes the surface temperature of Earth to rise.

Scientists know that using less fossil fuels is good for the environment. It slows global warming. Scientists are also concerned that Earth will run out of fossil fuels. They take millions of years to form in the ground. That means supply is limited.

Some drivers worry about the cost of gas as well. In the 1970s, oil producers in the Middle East were unhappy with the United States. They placed an oil **embargo** on the country. This ban caused gas prices to skyrocket. There were long lines at gas stations. Some gas stations would only let drivers buy a small amount of gas. Other gas stations ran out of gas completely! This was frustrating for drivers.

Today, **turmoil** in oil-producing nations makes the price of gas go up and down. It's no wonder people are switching to EVs!

oil pumps

TECHNOLOGY

Hybrid Vehicles

Hybrid vehicles are powered by *both* gasoline and electricity. A hybrid's main engine is powered by gas. It is used for higher speeds. A hybrid also has an electric motor attached to the engine. It is used for lower speeds. When the car needs extra power to go up hills, it uses both engines. Hybrids use less fuel than regular cars. They produce fewer emissions, too.

A gas station in Detroit tells drivers it has run out of gas in 1978.

SORRY OUT OF GAS!

SUPER REGULAR
Unleaded

Modern EVs

There are three main components of an EV. They are the battery, the controller, and the electric motor. When an EV is started, an electrical current passes from the battery to the controller. The controller manages the flow of electricity to the motor. It controls the speed of the motor. The motor sends the energy to the EV's transmission. The transmission powers the EV's axles. The axles turn the wheels. This makes the EV move.

Most EVs use battery packs made with lithium ions. They are like the batteries in smartphones. An EV just uses a lot more! EV batteries are lighter than other rechargeable batteries. They are located under the car's cabin. EV batteries are expensive. They can cost almost half as much as the car.

There is also a small battery under the hood of an EV. It powers the EV's accessories. That includes the windshield wipers and lights.

EVs have charge ports. Ports connect EVs to power supplies. The power supply can come from a wall socket. The battery takes about six to eight hours to recharge.

EV battery pack

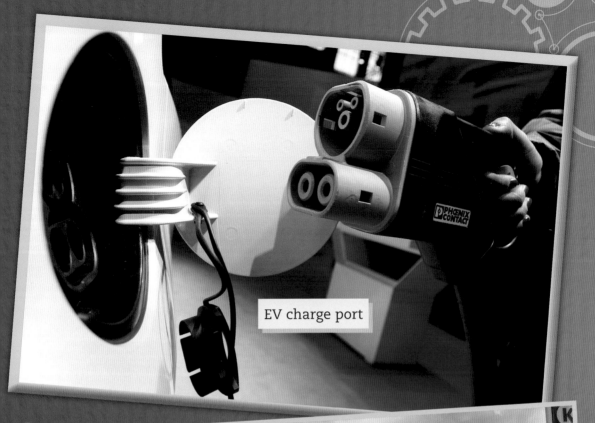

EV charge port

Tesla has created Supercharger stations that can partially charge EVs in just 15 minutes.

EVs look like cars that use gas, but they feel different to drive. Unlike noisy gas-powered cars, EVs are almost silent. There is no engine vibration. All you hear is the sound of the tires on the pavement and the slight whine of the motor when you accelerate.

EVs accelerate quickly. The Tesla Model S can go from 0 to 97 kmh (0 to 60 mph) in 2.28 seconds! That is because EVs have more **torque** (TORK) than gas-powered cars. Torque helps a car accelerate.

When driving an EV, drivers don't have to move their feet between the brake and the accelerator as often as they would in a gas car. When a foot is lifted off the accelerator, an EV slows quickly. It rolls to a stop by itself. Sometimes, drivers don't have to use the brakes at all. EV fans call this "one-pedal driving."

When drivers pump the brakes, they recharge the battery. This is called regenerative braking. It helps EVs get more miles on a single charge. Some people love driving EVs so much, they say they will never go back to gas cars!

ENGINEERING

Lighten Up

Gas-powered cars weigh a lot because they are made with heavy steel. Engineers did not want to use steel to make EVs. They already had large, heavy battery packs weighing them down. The lighter the EV, the longer it could drive on a single charge. Today's EVs use lightweight aluminum to make parts like the **chassis** (CHA-see), hood, and doors.

Tesla Model S electric engine on a chassis

In the past, EVs were pricey. A big reason for the high
[co]st was the battery. Lithium-ion batteries were expensive.
[Re]cent advances in battery technology, such as making them
[mo]re efficient, have lowered EV prices. Many countries
[off]er tax breaks to people who buy EVs. These tax breaks
[can] save people thousands of dollars. This means an EV can
[cos]t about the same as a car that uses gas. More people can
[affo]rd EVs!

[Ju]st like gas-powered cars, there are different kinds of
[EVs.] Some models are very expensive. There are also more
[basi]c models that cost less.

[Th]e Rolls-Royce Electric Phantom is a high-priced EV. It
[has m]ore features than most other EVs. But, it costs nearly a
[half] a million dollars to own!

[Mo]re affordable options are available. For example, the
[Nissa]n Leaf is a lot smaller than the Rolls-Royce Electric
[Phan]tom. But it has features, such as a solar panel on the
[roo]f, which powers the radio. Nowadays, every driver can
[find t]heir perfect EV.

[Rolls-R]oyce
[Electric] Phantom

EV Artists

Elon Musk, manufacturer of the Tesla EV, once posted a sketch of a unicorn online. He drew it on the touchpad of his EV. All Tesla touchpads have this hidden feature. Tap the T on the Tesla logo three times and the screen turns into a sketchpad. When you finish, the car asks, "Are you sure you want Tesla to critique your artistic masterpiece?" Then, you can publish your work.

Plugging In

Before people can drive an EV, they must charge its battery pack. Many people use a home charger.

An EV has a charging port, which is usually located on the driver's side or on the front of the car. One end of a cord plugs into the port, and the other end plugs into a power source. The electricity flows to the battery via an onboard charger. Then, a driver waits. It takes six to eight hours to recharge the batteries.

There are three main ways drivers charge their EVs. The first is the trickle charge. That is when they plug the EV into a standard electrical outlet. It is the slowest way to charge an EV.

The second way is to use an Electrical Vehicle Supply Equipment unit, or an **EVSE**. It is a box with a cord that supplies electricity to the EV. It is usually mounted on a garage wall.

The third way to refuel an EV is at a public charging station. Some governments provide them for free. Others are owned by businesses. They require drivers to pay for the electricity.

If your house loses electricity, you may be able to use your EV as a generator. Some models have power outlets.

The *range* of an EV is how far it can drive on the power from a full charge. Many EVs have a range of over 160 km (100 mi.). Most people drive less than this each day. This means EVs are becoming more practical.

The **median** range that EVs can travel without a recharge is about 185 km (115 mi.). This range continues to grow with new EVs, but it still falls short of gas cars. Gas cars have a median range of about 660 km (410 mi.) before drivers need to stop for fuel.

How far an EV can go depends on the car model and the size of its battery pack. The car's speed and the number of hills climbed are also factors. It takes more energy for a car to drive up a mountain.

There is a charge **gauge** on the dashboard. It tells an EV driver how much power the car has left in the battery. The power is shown as a percentage. A full charge is 100 percent. If it reads 10 percent, it's time to plug in. EV drivers need to be good at **estimating** how far a car's power level will let them travel.

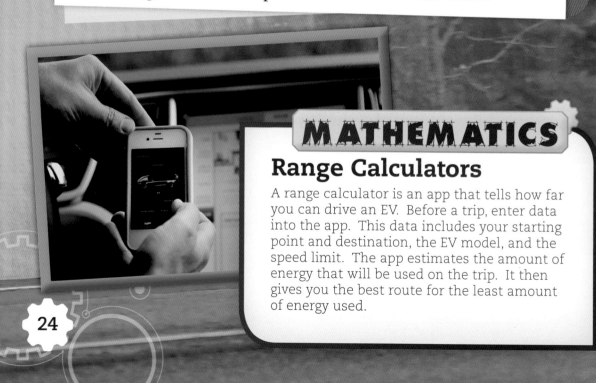

MATHEMATICS

Range Calculators

A range calculator is an app that tells how far you can drive an EV. Before a trip, enter data into the app. This data includes your starting point and destination, the EV model, and the speed limit. The app estimates the amount of energy that will be used on the trip. It then gives you the best route for the least amount of energy used.

"Range anxiety" is a nervous feeling some EV drivers get when they are not sure that they have enough power to get to their destination.

Some EVs, such as the Tesla Model S (shown), can drive nearly 550 km (340 mi.) on a single charge.

The Future of EVs

Exciting new EV models are introduced every year. They are being sold at lower prices as batteries become cheaper to make. One day, an EV could cost less than a car that can be filled at a gas pump.

This makes people who care about the environment happy. They are eager to buy EVs. They don't want to drive cars that produce smog and air pollution. They want to do their part to reduce global warming.

Countries around the world have begun to encourage their citizens to drive EVs. Public charging stations are popping up everywhere. The United Kingdom and France plan to ban the sale of new cars that use gas by 2040.

Engineers are working on ways to make EVs more efficient. They have placed solar panels on EVs. They are experimenting with wind power. They are studying ways to install electrical currents in roads. The currents could power EVs as they speed along the highway. EVs look like they could be the cars of the future!

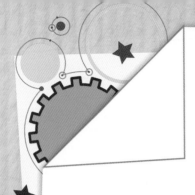

STEAM CHALLENGE

Define the Problem

Engineers often try to make products work in new ways. Your task is to build a model car that can drive 2 meters (6.5 feet) along a flat surface without being pushed.

Constraints: You may use no more than five of the following items to build your car: cardboard, pencils, rubber bands, paper clips, straws, craft sticks, balloons, plastic bottles, plastic bottle caps, glue, and tape.

Criteria: Your model car must move forward at least 2 m (6.5 ft.) along a flat surface without being pushed.

Research and Brainstorm

What are some ways a car can be powered to move forward? What parts does a car need to have?

Design and Build

Sketch your design. What materials will you choose? Why did you choose these materials? Build the model.

Test and Improve

Mark two lines on the floor 2 m (6.5 ft.) apart. Place your car on one line and test whether you can get it to drive over the second. Did it work? What changes might improve the car's performance? Revise your model and try again.

Reflect and Share

Would your car be successful if the lines were 3 m (10 ft.) apart? Can your car drive up an incline?

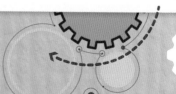

Glossary

cancer—a group of diseases that involve abnormal cell growth

chassis—the base frame of a car

crude—very simple and basic

ecosystems—the groups of living and nonliving things that make up an environment

embargo—an official ban on trade or business activities

emission—the discharge of something, such as a gas

estimating—roughly calculating the amount of something

EVSE—electric vehicle supply equipment; a type of charging unit for electric vehicles

fossil fuels—fuels, such as coal, oil, or natural gas, that are made from dead plants or animals

gauge—an instrument that measures the amount of something

industrialist—a person involved in the ownership or management of industry

median—the middle value in a series of values arranged from smallest to largest

port—a place for being physically connected to another device

spew—expel large quantities of something

spoiler—a device on the back of a car designed to reduce air drag

torque—a type of force that measures changes in the rotational speed of an object

toxins—organic poisons

turmoil—a state of confusion or disorder

VIPs—very important persons

Index

aluminum, 19

Anderson, Robert, 8

Electrobat, 10

Ford, Henry, 10

greenhouse gases, 6–7, 14

lead-acid batteries, 9

lithium-ion battery, 4, 20

Middle East, 14

Model T, 10–11

Morrison, William, 8–9

Musk, Elon, 21

New York City, 10

Nissan Leaf, 20

Planté, Gaston, 9

Rimac Concept One, 5

Rolls-Royce Phantom, 20

solar panel, 20, 26

Tesla, 17–19, 21, 25

Do you want to engineer EVs?
Here are some tips to get you started.

"Invention is the development of a new idea. Innovation is improving something that already exists. Creating a modern electric car demonstrated both and the challenges of those processes. Always look for ways to invent and innovate!"—*Susan Tolbert, Museum Curator*

"Knowing the history of things helps you better understand them and the role they played in history. For example, electric cars were advertised as 'ladies' cars' in the 1900s. Many men thought women lacked the mental ability and physical strength to drive gasoline-powered cars. By learning about history, you can work to make better inventions. You can also make the world better by avoiding the stereotypes of the past."—*Roger White, Museum Curator*